Your Exodus Is At Hand

Bondage doesn't have to last forever!

Dianne Clark Clayton

ISBN 979-8-89345-419-2 (paperback)
ISBN 979-8-89345-420-8 (digital)

Christian Faith Publishing
832 Park Avenue
Meadville, PA 16335
www.christianfaithpublishing.com

Printed in the United States of America

My Confession About my exodus came about after getting a CD from Jerry Savelle titled *Your Exodus Has Begun!* while I was going through a difficult season in my life. "My exodus has come" was my confession when it seemed like it wasn't going to happen, but the LORD brought me out into my promised land. I have used the Old Testament Bible story of the Israelites' exodus from Egypt after four hundred years of bondage to be a reference for my story. I wasn't in bondage as long as the Israelites were, but at times, it seemed like it was going to go on forever. *But God* was once again faithful in my life and delivered me. There was a saying, "If God has delivered you, why should you be bound?" The Second Book of Corinthians 2:14 states, "Now thanks be unto GOD, which always causeth us to triumph in CHRIST." Writing this book is part of that victory that HE has given me through CHRIST JESUS. GLORY HALLELUJAH!

CONTENTS

I Am Announcing to you now that your exodus from bondage is at hand. You might be in bondage from alcoholism, drug addiction, pornography, abuse of all kinds, poverty, gluttony, or anything that is holding you hostage preventing you from fulfilling your GOD-ordained destiny. I want you to know that bondage has a time limit in the Kingdom of GOD. When HE says that the time of your exodus is at hand, then that settles it. You need to get in agreement with HIM and be ready to walk out of that bondage now. Glory hallelujah!

In the Bible days, a group of people called the Israelites were in bondage in Egypt for hundreds of years. At first, when their ancestors got to Egypt, the Israelites were guests of Joseph, who was prime minister of Egypt at that time. Joseph was born in Israel and was sold into slavery by his brothers to a group of people called the Midianites for twenty pieces of silver. Then the Midianites took Jospeh to Egypt, where he was sold to Potiphar, the captain of the guard of Pharaoh. After many years, Joseph died, and the Pharaoh, following his death, knew him not. This new Pharaoh was concerned about how the Israelites had increased more in number and in more power than them. So he put them in bondage and had the taskmasters to afflict them with their burdens to build their cities. Thank GOD, this was not the end of their story. Bondage is also not the end of your story.

First Things First

You Might Be wondering what this story has to do with you. Your exodus is at hand. Like me, you might have been in bondage for years. It doesn't matter the time frame when GOD is in the picture. As long as you are breathing, there is always an opportunity to change the ending to your life's story. With GOD, all things are possible. So, yes, GOD has an exodus for you. Be encouraged and get ready for it. First, if you haven't given your life to GOD by accepting HIS Son, JESUS, do it now. John 3:16 states, "For GOD so loved the world, that HE gave HIS only begotten Son (JESUS), that whosoever believeth in HIM should not perish, but have everlasting life." Romans 10:9–10 states, "That if thou shalt confess with thy mouth the LORD JESUS, and shalt believe in thine heart that GOD hath raised HIM (JESUS) from the dead, thou shalt be saved. For with the heart man believeth unto righteousness; and with the mouth confession is made unto salvation." If you have sincerely believed the above truth and confessed this, you are saved.

Welcome to the family of GOD! Salvation was the first step, but the next step is to be baptized with the HOLY GHOST and with fire! Just like you received your salvation by faith, ask JESUS to baptize you with the HOLY GHOST and with fire by like faith and receive it by faith. This encounter will empower you to live a victorious life in CHRIST JESUS and be effective in your GOD-ordained purpose. Every day, ask JESUS to purge you of all things not like HIM and refill you with the HOLY GHOST and with fire. You are on your way out of bondage and on your way into your GOD-ordained promised land.

Chapter 2

Background of the Israelites' Exodus

Let's Move On talking about how your exodus is at hand. Referring back to the Israelites, their exodus did finally come after many, many years. God sent them a deliverer by the name of Moses. He was born in Egypt many years before God sent him back there to bring the Israelites out of bondage. They had cried to God for their deliverance, and He heard their prayers. In His perfect timing, God answered their prayers and manifested their exodus from Egypt. He will do the same thing for you like He did for them and me. Hallelujah, bless His name! So, be of good cheer.

By faith, take your prayer of petition to the Lord about wanting to exit your current situation of bondage. That situation is only temporary in the sight of God! Believe that He has heard your prayer and has answered it too. Yes, God will manifest your exodus from the land of bondage like He did for the Israelites from Egypt. Take it from me, it will happen. Stay in faith no matter what it looks like. Expect it to happen suddenly. My God is the God of "suddenlies." Nothing is too hard for Him.

Back to the Israelites. Moses finally said yes to God's call to deliver His chosen people. At first, Moses didn't think He could be a deliverer because of a speech problem. So God let him know that He would be with him, and He also sent Aaron (his brother) with him to be his spokesperson. They both worked together to deliver the Israelites.

One time Moses asked God, "Behold, when I come unto the children of Israel and shall say unto them, 'The God of your fathers hath sent me unto you,' and they shall say to me, 'What is His name?' what shall I say unto them?"

And God said unto Moses, "I Am that I Am," and He said, "Thus shalt thou say unto the children of Israel, I Am hath sent me unto you." Today, I feel that God want me to tell you that "I Am that I Am is with you and will deliver you from all bondage from the enemy."

My God is well able to bring you out from where you are today to bring you into your promised land. Be encouraged, your exodus is at hand.

Next in the Bible story, Moses showed up with his brother, Aaron, in Egypt. God told Moses to say to the children of Israel, "I Am hath sent Me unto you. The Lord God of your fathers, the God of Abraham, the God of Isaac, and the God of Jacob hath sent Me unto you; this is My name forever, and this is My memorial unto all generations." God knows just what to say to us His children when we need a new word.

You know that the devil isn't going to want you to be loosed from his grip, but he has got to let you go. Hold your ground in faith because your exodus is at hand! Grab hold of a scripture of deliverance and believe, receive, and confess it by faith until you see the manifestation. No matter what it looks like in the natural, by faith it is already done in the Spirit. Your deliverance has been paid for by Jesus, now and henceforth.

Well, the first time that Moses and Aaron met with Pharaoh and told him, "Thus said the Lord God of Israel, let my people go, that they may hold a feast unto Me in the wilderness," God had hardened Pharaoh's heart. So, Pharaoh did not honor their request. Also, Pharaoh increased the labor of the Israelites men. Thank God, this story didn't end here. God is always faithful to His word.

Chapter 3

Plagues of Egypt

Well, It Took GOD performing many plagues to come upon the Egyptian people, livestock, and land before Pharaoh let the Israelites go. The first plague was that all the Egyptian water was changed into blood. On the other hand, The Israelites' water was perfectly fine in their land of Goshen. Next, the second plague was that of frogs overrunning the Egyptian land and homes, but the Israelites were not bothered with them. The third plague consisted of the dust of the ground turning into lice all over the land of Egypt, but the land of Goshen had none. Furthermore, the fourth plague was swarms of flies sent upon the houses and land of Egypt, but once again, the land of Goshen had none. Still, Pharaoh did not let the Israelites go after all this turmoil these fourth plagues had caused him and his people.

Moreover, the fifth plague consisted of the death of all the Egyptians' livestock, including the cattle, horses, asses, camels, oxen, and sheep, but none of the Israelites' livestock died. Then, the sixth plague brought boils which broke forth with blains upon all the Egyptian people and their beasts. Soon the seventh plague followed with hail mingled with fire. Both the Egyptian people and their beasts were smitten. The eighth plague was locusts that covered all the land where the Egyptians lived. The locusts ate all the fruit of the trees that the hail had left. There was no green thing on the trees or in the herbs of the field. Furthermore, the whole land was darkened by all the locusts. Once again, Pharaoh's heart was hardened in spite of the locusts, and he did not let the Israelites leave.

In regard to the ninth plague, there was darkness that was thick and lasted three days in all the land of the Egyptians. They did not see one another for those three days of complete darkness. Last, but not least, the tenth plague followed. This final plague came with the death of the firstborn of every Egyptian and their beasts. The Israelites' children were not touched. To avoid the death angel, they were told to put blood on their lintel and the two side posts of their homes. Finally, Pharaoh's heart changed, and he made the decision to let the Israelites go. They were finally released from bondage. Yes, their exodus was finally a reality.

Chapter 4

Make a Plan

Another Key To your exodus is making a plan. I had someone advising me about my exodus. She said, "You need to make a plan." So I started making a plan. I didn't have much time to complete and get things in order for my exodus, *But God* knew the ending from the beginning. Not everything worked out so smooth, but here I am, still thankful unto God first and then everyone else who helped me during this exodus. To add, my saying was, "Thank God for everything and everyone He has used to get me to where I am now!" I am still enjoying my exodus. Glory hallelujah!

Next, since you have made Jesus your Lord and Savior and have been baptized with the Holy Ghost and with fire, you need to seek God about His direction concerning your exodus. God will probably tell you to get at least one scripture to stand on in faith while you are believing for your exodus. For example, He might tell you to confess by faith, Joel 2:32: "And it shall come to pass, that whosoever shall call on the name of The Lord shall be delivered." You might pray that word in faith, believing, and your exodus happens just like that. On the other hand, it might be that God tells you to go to a certain church where people are serving in deliverance ministry, and they can pray over you to break that bondage. Maybe, you might have to seek out one of your faith-believing friends that can contend in prayer for your deliverance from the bondage you are in. Just like that, God can deliver you from years of bondage through that agreement prayer of faith. In contrast, you might also have to go through a process like I did to receive your deliverance from bondage. GOD might tell you to fast and pray for five days, start saving extra money, have your suitcase already packed and hidden, change your job, or disconnect from negative friendships.

Whatever HE says, do it! I say, believe for the "now" deliverance from bondage because faith is in the now, according to Hebrews 11:1. If it doesn't come that suddenly, stay in faith, be patient, and be obedient unto GOD to whatever HE is showing you to do. Whatever your process is, whether it is now or whether it is a week or month from now before you experience your exodus, don't give up believing by faith! I want you to know that I am standing in the gap for you and cheering you on. "Your exodus is at hand!" Also, as my brother-in-CHRIST or sister-in-CHRIST, I am believing to see you in Glory Land one day which will be our ultimate promised land! GOD BLESS!

Chapter 5

Payback from the Enemy

Well, Even Though Pharaoh let the Israelites go, the story didn't end there. On another note, before they left Egypt, the Israelites didn't leave empty handed. God made their enemies repay them for the many years of serving with no pay. The Israelites borrowed of the Egyptians jewels of silver, jewels of gold, and raiment before they left. The Egyptians gave them such things as they required. The Israelites despoiled their slave owners.

When God brings you out of bondage, the devil will have to pay you back what he owes you. Proverbs 6:31 states, "But if he be found, he shall restore sevenfold; he shall give all the substance of his house." So, the devil owes you a whole lot. Claim that scripture by faith and expect to see the manifestation of it now and henceforth.

Conclusion

Finally, Getting To the ending of the Bible story of the exodus from Egypt, Pharaoh changed his mind after the Israelites were on their journey out of bondage. Pharaoh and his army pursued them all the way to the Red Sea. GOD had Moses perform another sign and wonder. Moses was told by GOD to stretch out his hand over the Red Sea and the waters divided, and the sea was made dry land. Almighty is our GOD. The children of Israel were able to cross on this dry land, but Pharaoh and his army had another fate. After they pursued after the Israelites, GOD told Moses to stretch out his hand over the sea again, and the water came again and drown Pharaoh and all his army. Praise GOD, Moses and the Israelites sang a song unto the LORD following this victory over their enemy. One of the verses of the victory song was, "The LORD is my strength and song, and HE is become my salvation: HE is my GOD… It was a glorious day!

When the enemy is made to let you go free, he might try to put you in bondage again if you let him. Hold fast to your victory by faith with corresponding action. Praise GOD for your victory in song, dance… however you want to show gratefulness unto HIM for bringing you out of bondage. Believe that GOD has your back in every unfavorable condition.

The conclusion of the exodus of the Israelites out of Egypt on their way to their promised land is a testimony of how faithful GOD is to HIS word. When GOD promises something, that puts the end to wondering. "It is a done deal." The Israelites did not come out of bondage just free, but they came out rich too, to the glory of GOD. Also, when all those plagues were brought upon the Egyptians, the Israelites, their land of Goshen, their livestock, and their beasts were not touched. GOD's people should be distinguished people in the middle of a dark place. The world should see GOD is with us, HIS children, and HE is taking care of all our needs.

Your exodus is at hand! You should no longer be a slave to anyone or anything if you are one of GOD's children. Praise and thank GOD in advance before your exodus occurs. Then, afterward, praise and thank HIM some more for the exodus when it happens. Do you feel a shout coming on now, just thinking about how Your Exodus is At Hand?

Next, don't forget to give your testimony about how GOD did it. Your testimony will help, strengthen, and encourage others who are still entangled in some form of bondage. Also, your testimony will give them hope of their exodus someday. It will motivate them to keep on believing, obeying HIS direction, and trusting GOD until it manifests. Proverbs 13:12 states, "Hope deferred maketh the heart sick; but when the desire cometh, it is a tree of life." So, always, as stated by Jessie Jackson, "keep hope alive." Hope is a powerful spiritual tool and weapon against the discouragement of the enemy and all his other evil tactics and strategies of bondage.

Well, the children of Israel did receive their freedom, and they were on their way to their promised land. Know that GOD doesn't bring you out of something bad not to bring you into something good. HE always sees the end from the beginning. HE is Alpha and Omega. GOD is always trying to get you to move forward in the plan HE has for your life, the abundant life. It's the thief, the devil, that comes to steal, kill, and destroy. On the other hand, JESUS came "that they might have life, and that they might have it more abundantly." Now, I hope you see that no matter how long you have been in bondage to something or someone, your exodus is at hand. Keep your eyes on the deliverer WHO is GOD and not on the person or thing that has held you as a hostage. GOD is faithful to bring you out. Hold on to your faith in HIM. HE will not let you down; HE is the unfailing GOD. HE has the best plan for your life, and it doesn't include bondage of any kind. If you going to be a bondservant to anyone or anything, let it be to GOD, WHO knew you before the foundation of the world and created you in HIS own image. GOD sent HIS only begotten Son, JESUS, to set you free. THEY both got your best interest in mind, and so do I. The deliverance that GOD provides will bring glory to HIMSELF, edify others, and be for your good.

After your exodus has come and gone, what is your next step? Continue to seek GOD every day and allow HIM to lead you by HIS Spirit. The HOLY SPIRIT will never lead you wrong. Freedom is yours after your exodus. When GOD has brought you out, never get entangled in that bondage again. I am congratulating you in advance on your exodus and your newfound freedom. "Greater Things in The LORD are Here and Now! Grab hold of it all by faith, and don't let go. Make the devil regret that he ever tangled with you in the first place. PRAISE THE LORD! YOUR EXODUS TRULY IS AT HAND!

Dianne Clark Clayton is a daughter of GOD with an evangelistic call and Deborah prophetic anointing. Also, GOD has graced her with other gifts as singing, writing songs, writing poems, teaching, etc. She gives GOD all the glory for allowing her to be used as a vessel chosen by HIM before the foundation of the world. Her heart's desire is to please HIM in all she does and says. Dianne wants to encourage the saints to come up higher in GOD and the sinners to make JESUS their LORD and SAVIOR above all. "The Great Awakening is Here and Now All Across The Nations! Greater Things in The LORD are Here and Now All Across The Nations! JESUS is coming Again Soon, and We All Need to BE READY!"

At the writing of this book, Dianne is separated and living out the purpose GOD has called her to and pressing toward the fulfillment of it. She has a dear son, a lovely daughter-in-love, and one precious grandson. She looks forward to love being called G-Mama by her grandson. She lives in a small town, Hernando, Mississippi, that is steadily growing with people, subdivisions, and new businesses. Dianne Praises and Thanks GOD for the publishing and the readers of her book which she believes were preordained by HIM, for HIS glory, for their edification, and for her good. GOD BLESS!